Obedience

Obedience

The *Key* to *Unlocking* God's Faithfulness

Lurline Grant

RESTORATION OF THE BREACH
WITHOUT BORDERS

ISBN: 978-1-954755-80-2

Published by:
Restoration of the Breach without Borders
West Palm Beach, Florida 33407
restorativeauthor@gmail.com
Tele: (475) 233 9008

Dedication

This book is dedicated to the glory of God and to
everyone who desires to walk in greater levels
of obedience to His will.

Foreword

Obedience is the fruit of the believer's love for God, and this journey of denying our way to follow Him is rewarded by His communion with us. Jesus puts it this way as He concluded His ministry to His core disciples *"If you keep my commandments, you will abide in my love, just as I have kept my Father's commandments and abide in his love."* (John 15:10 ESV)

"Obedience, the Key to Unlocking God's Faithfulness" is a demonstration of the author's commitment to this revelation. This book is fruit that she holds the beauty of submission and obedience to her Father in high regard. Dr. Grant, who I affectionately call Aunty Lurline, has put together in potent and practical language the necessity of the believer to walk in responsiveness to God and His loving reply to this lifestyle.

You will be carried on a journey that depicts authentic communion with God filled with the ebbs and flows of life. Within these passages is captured a heart that has grown acquainted with the voice of her Father and plastered along each chapter is a challenge for the reader to do the same.

A teacher by nature, Dr. Grant breaks down scriptural concepts to point us in the direction of why God commands obedience, the different ways our obedience can be manifested, and the radical ways God uses our submission.

In the conversation that led to me writing this foreword, my aunt said, "I believe this book is for this generation and the generation to come." That pierced my heart because I often admire women my aunt and mother's age for their steadiness with the Lord and how in mundanity and excitement, they have kept the course in following and responding to Jesus.

This book is for those of us who want a glimpse into what a life lived with Jesus looks like throughout the decades. This book is riddled with testimonies for you if you have cowered in disobedience because you feared what was on the other side of your yes. This written piece of ministry is for the heart that needs to be warmed by the reminders of God's faithfulness to us when we are faithful to Him.

Carefully go over these pages and earnestly pant after a heart of obedience. I pray that in reading these words you will be confronted but also gifted the grace to pursue wholehearted devotion and submission to your Father.

-Jhonelle Grant Fitz-Henley
Christian Writer

Contents

Acknowledgments

Very special thanks to Pastor Dr. Leostone Morrison and his wife Sherene Morrison. It is their gifts of discernment and willing obedience that have brought a Rhema word to life. I thank God for your ministry and may it accomplish all that God has predestined for it to do in the earth.

Special thanks with lots of gratitude to my Pastor, Teacher, and confidant Apostle Dr. Althea Grant, whose love and stern mentorship are at the crux of my walking in obedience to God's calling for my life regardless of where it takes me. Thank You.

Thanks to my family who are always supportive of me. To my sister Jenn who never ceases to give those gentle loving reminders of the task that is at hand.

My son Colwyn who encourages and spot checks me in every area of my life including this book.

My niece Jhonelle, whose oversight brought structure and clarity to my expression.

Thanks to My HAPEM family whose love and prayers I could not exist without.

To Sigrid Wardlaw whose "You can do it" Cheers stimulated the confidence I needed for this. . . .

To my friend Marcia Parker whose confident assurance is a pillar of strength.

Thanks to you, my readers. It's your heart that God has responded to.

Preface

*W*hat does God require of us? In his book "The Secret of the Stairs" Pastor Wade E. Taylor said, "To be obedient to God speaks of us having a 'Spirit of obedience' resident within us that responds with unquestioning obedience to his request". (The Secret of the Stairs pg. 69). When we come into that place of willing obedience, it will bring us into a position of an intimate relationship with our God- which will give Him the right to take us into situations where there's no choice but to get to know the benefits of His faithfulness. Our unwavering yes to God indicates a wholehearted trust in His divine character and the manifestation of it in whatever our situation might be. God being completely faithful is one of His moral attributes. Moral because it is a part of Himself that He reveals and desires to share with us as we walk in a relationship with Him. My sharing of these testimonies and encounters is an attempt to walk in obedience to what I believe God desires me to do in this season of my life.

Chapter 1
Can God Trust You to Be Obedient?

"I can't believe you didn't let me realize that God had heard my prayers. Yesterday was very hard for me; I only had things to make porridge for us to eat."

an God trust you to be obedient to carry out His request? There are times when God will not issue a command and say go ye and do this - He will just simply tell or ask us to do something unexpected; something that does not even make sense; something that might even cause us to think that others will doubt that God sent us, and they might even ridicule us for having followed His instruction.

Case in point

One evening after a church meeting, a group of us had gone to visit a friend's house. She gave each of us a small packet of cinnamon leaves and reminded us how great this spice was for adding flavor to teas and porridges. However, to our sister Joyce, she gave two packets and bid us farewell.

When I got home, I put mine away in the cupboard and forgot about it until one particular Sunday morning when the Lord had need of it. There I was rushing to share breakfast so my son and I could eat before leaving for church. Then right in the middle of my activities, I felt that familiar nudge, and I heard in my spirit, "God, why would I take cinnamon leaves to her now? Remember, she was the person who received the most when our friend gave them out?" I even said to myself, "Here I am having eggs and sausage for breakfast, and I'm giving her cinnamon leaves as if to say, 'I hope this will make your porridge breakfast taste better.'" At that moment, I worried that she might think I was looking down on her and her family.

It is widely believed in Jamaica where I am from, that porridge as a meal is for someone who is poor or has come up on some real hard times or might be recovering from an ailment. So, I did not obey. I could never have insulted her that way. My thought then was, if I couldn't give eggs and sausage like I was having, then I should leave her be.

In the afternoon, when I got home after church, the very same thing happened. While sharing my dinner, there came that nudge in my spirit. I heard the Holy Spirit saying, "Take some cinnamon leaves down to your friend." This time, I was even more disobedient. I said, "Lord no, she's going to believe that I'm saying she should only have porridge for dinner." I looked in my pot and realized the chicken I had cooked for dinner wouldn't be enough to share among us and her grandchildren, or at least that's what I believed. So once again, I disobeyed.

However, let it not be said that I did not obey the Lord. So, in my **fleshly attempt** to be obedient, I packed the cinnamon leaves in my pocketbook and took them with me the Monday evening to church as we were having a special meeting. While walking to the meeting my friend Joyce turned and said to me, "Lurline, yesterday was a hard Sunday for me. The only thing I had in the house to eat was some cornmeal and a little bit of sugar and salt to make porridge." She said "The place was so empty, and I had no money. The grandchildren and I had porridge for breakfast and dinner. Girl, I said to the Lord, "God, if you could just give me some cinnamon leaves to spice up this porridge, I would feel a little better." As she shared her story, I became so broken and very sorrowful. Her words weighed very heavily on my heart. I was hurting because I realized how disobedient I had been to God. I singlehandedly became the obstacle that broke the communication flow between God and one of His prized possessions. This precious child whom He was given an opportunity to experience true intimacy with Him had been robbed of the blessedness of coming into the understanding of the immeasurable faithfulness of our Heavenly Father.

She was deprived of living out the testimony of Matthew 7:9-11 which tells us that, *"the Heavenly Father will not give us a snake if we ask for fish, and neither would he give us stones if we ask for bread."* This same verse lets us know that He provides even better than our earthly fathers do.

I put my hand in the bag, pulled out the packet of cinnamon leaves, and handed it to her while weeping. I told her what God had said to me before I had my breakfast and before I had my dinner the day before. She strongly rebuked me and said, "I can't believe you did not let me realize that God had heard and answered my prayers." She said, "Yesterday was very hard for me, I only had things to make that porridge for us to eat- which did not taste so good."

She said, "When I tasted it, I turned and told God if He would give me some cinnamon leaves to spice it up, I would be grateful." All this time I was crying my eyes out and wishing that the earth would open and take me in.

I asked for forgiveness from both her and our Heavenly Father. Not long after, I heard the voice of the Lord speaking again into my spirit. He said, "No flesh shall glory in my Glory. In all these ways (and many more), God will be glorified." He also said, *"I will not give my glory to another" (Isaiah 48:11).*

I realized there and then that in my fleshly endeavors not to insult my friend, I had robbed God of His opportunity to be glorified in her praises. Additionally, I single-handedly railroaded a prime opportunity for someone to testify of God's goodness and faithfulness.

Takeaway

Your obedience is the answer to someone's prayer.

Chapter 2
All Is Required!

"But this is what I commanded them, saying, 'Obey My voice, and I will be your God, and you shall be My people. And walk in all the ways that I have commanded you, that it may be well with you.' "Jeremiah 7:23

*F*or us to have abundance and success in every area of our lives, we must choose to be obedient to the written or spoken word of the Lord our God. God's plan for me to migrate to the USA was working its way into the depths of my spirit. The details of my being called to the United States and subsequent testimonies are presented in other chapters of this book.

In order to fully prepare I started saving heavily. The time for me to leave was fast approaching. I had no idea how my son would survive. Yes, he was over 20 years old, but he was in his last semester in college, and he had not yet been established in a job so he would definitely need money. My plan was to leave him with enough money to cover the fundamentals such as mortgage, food, etc. I sacrificed everything

6

that I could and poured it into my savings. There was no way I was going to leave him uncared for. He and I sat down and discussed the plan of action for what was ahead of us. During this time of planning, I didn't think I needed God's help.

The Word clearly states that it's the parent's duty to leave a blessing for their children. *"A good man leaves an inheritance to his children's children." (Proverbs 13:22 NKJV).* Therefore, there was no way I would leave him without figuring out how to keep the roof over his head. My plan to preserve him was in full force. I had now saved up enough money to cover about six month's expenses. I had read that we should try to save a minimum of six months' salary to take us through any rough times we might come upon. Remember I told you that I had left God out of this part of the planning? I never asked Him what to do or how I was to protect or invest the money I had saved for my son. All I kept doing was to drop in a few begging prayers at His feet, in between my flurry of activities to ensure that the money would come together, and it did. Praise be to God! Jehovah Jireh faithfully brought the provision that made it all come together.

Now I knew for sure that this was what He desired me to do. Yes, His hand was at work. Because in my mind I felt that I had submitted to Him and was poised to experience the blessings that He gives to those who are obedient. It was now a couple of days before my scheduled departure, and I was using the dragging method of obedience. Dragging by taking my own sweet time to make my travel plans. I booked a ticket for Friday the 29th of August for the last flight on the last day of August 2003. This was in obedience to God's Word in which He told me that I should migrate to the USA and join my youngest sister in ministry and that I was to do so before August ends. In trying to maintain my relationship with my heavenly Father, I tried not to argue about the timing of my departure. However, I found myself behaving somewhat like a child whose dad had told them to turn off the television and go to bed.

I was moving very slowly on everything regarding my departure. Just like a delinquent child who might slowly slide out of the chair, turn over on their tummy then get on their knees, and even more slowly raise up to stand. Then slowly searched for the remote and paused for another few minutes before actually turning off the TV. This is the best way I can describe how I dragged myself out of Jamaica while trying to obey the Lord. I was hurting at the thought of leaving my son, especially at a time when he was about to graduate from college. But, let me not get ahead of myself. During the week before I left, my church went on a week of fasting and prayer. I was all prayed up and listening for my directives. Looking back in hindsight, what God had told me to do that week was the best money-earning plan I could have invested in. Please, do not get me wrong, I was not skipping with God through the tulips on this idea. I thought it was a bad idea, in fact, I thought it was a very bad one. How could a loving God have asked this of me? He knew I had only one child and was a single parent with no real backup plan.

Yet, He insisted that I give away all the money I had saved to take care of my son. "Why Lord?" I asked Him, "Why?" What kind of mother would people think I was?" Yet, He assured me that He had this. Though He allowed my son to be confirmed in his job before I left, I was still not fully persuaded. I asked, "God! Why would you want me to look so uncaring?" But thanks be to God, He gave me a son who always supported me in my desire to obey the Lord. He never took me on a guilt trip for obeying God and being separated from him at this point of transitioning in his life. Yet, he was in full agreement with God's plan, even though it meant I would not be at his college graduation. Now, be reminded that I was in fasting and prayer with my church. I was also using this time to really submit myself to hearing God's heart. He did speak to me. It was in this time of being yielded that God revealed the plan of giving all the money I had saved to someone who was in need. His plan was that the recipient of His blessing was my best friend in the church.

As close as we were she never told me all her financial woes. I guess that was between her and God. The Holy Spirit told me to call her and take her to lunch the next day. I said, "Lunch? We are fasting!" As if He didn't know that. He instructed me to purchase soup for both of us, considering it was a liquid fast anyway. Now, isn't it just like our Heavenly Father to cover all the bases? I made the call and asked her if we could do our one liquid meal at a restaurant the next day. She questioned, "Lunch? Aren't we fasting? I told her that we could order a soup without meat etc, to which she agreed. We got together and our lunch date had a cloud hanging over it the whole time. It was the kind of heaviness that comes with the sadness of impending separation. We were fully aware that we may never do this again, or if we did, it would not be any time soon.

Our emotions were right there on our sleeves, so we wept a bit. The lunch was delicious as usual. We chatted about what we perceived God was doing in my life with His migration plan. As our time of fellowship was coming to an end, I told her that God said I was to give her the money I saved. That's when the tsunami of tears came. Mine, because this was definitely a whole new level of obedience. I had to trust God for the well-being of my son without my input. For my friend, it was the knowledge of knowing how big a sacrifice it was for me, and that God would choose to favor her that way. The best part of this story was that while my friend was preparing to meet me for lunch, the Lord told her that she should gather all the bills that she had been praying to Him about and take them with her. She had no idea what God was going to do. She thought we were going to intercede over them.

So, like many well-meaning Christians sometimes do, she didn't want to burden the Lord with everything. Therefore, she brought the more outstanding bills and left the rest at home. When I told her what God said and gave her the money, she realized that God had covered everything including the ones she left at home. She gave Him praise and said that He wiped her debt slate clean.

Her **partial obedience** (by not taking all her bills to our lunch meeting) had no impact on God's complete faithfulness. The Holy Spirit then spoke to my heart and said, "Now that your seed is planted, I can make ready your harvest". That's when it started to make sense to me- **Obedience is always the key to unlocking God's faithfulness.**

Let me testify here, not only did God allow my son to meet his expenses but he paid off the mortgage on the house and gave me the title one year as a Christmas gift. The Scripture tells us that there is a joy that awaits those who sow in tears.

"Those who sow in tears shall reap in joy. He who continually goes forth weeping, bearing seed for sowing, shall doubtless come again with rejoicing, Bringing his sheaves with him". (Psalm 126: 5-6)

Also, let us never forget the promises in Deuteronomy 28:1-14 for those who are obedient to God.

God has promised blessings for those who obey Him.

Chapter 3
The Price of Disobedience

*M*any well-intended children of God find themselves walking in disobedience to the will of God in order to secure themselves. Just like Moses and Jonah, who chose responses that would keep their reputation intact, we sometimes flow from the place of our emotions. Although we often know from the scriptures what God requires, we might choose to appease the spirit of pride. When I was faced with this decision, I too opted to save my face.

This happened when I was deeply hurt by someone. Although I knew the Christlike thing to do was to forgive completely, I tried with everything in me to forgive on my terms. My plan was to avoid the person as best as possible. I thought staying out of range would be good enough, but the Lord used my pastor to let me know that I was functioning from a place of appeasement.

Seeking to portray the image that all was well, my great plan was to be a good Christian and not walk in a way that would not open me up to more hurt from the person. But God wanted me to live at the place of total forgiveness "as if it never happened." Living from the place of true Godly forgiveness. However, there was a part of me that struggled with the fear of being hurt again. The thought of that situation reoccurring had me trapped and soon disobedience became the choice of my free will. In my opinion, all I wanted to do was play it safe. Notwithstanding, that act of disobedience opened the door for fear to enter my heart. Fear brought feelings of resentment. Thanks be to God; I was delivered before hatred could make its way in.

It's easy to choose disobedience when obedience leaves us vulnerable to hurt and pain. Yet, our Lord and Savior Jesus, knowing all this, made the choice of obedience. We, too, are all called to take up our cross daily and walk the walk of obedience. May God strengthen us all to do this. There is indeed a balm in Gilead to heal our wounded souls and He will make us whole; Our Jehovah Rapha is faithful.

I must confess that this is my least favorite part of this book. However, it must be a part of the book. Although I would rather highlight God's faithfulness to the obedient, there will be those who choose not to obey. Another reality is that we all find ourselves in that group at some point, especially before we understand the value of a loving, obedient relationship with God. The

Bible does teach us that disobedience has its reward as well, and because God is the faithful, just judge, He will equally acknowledge and address our disobedience. One of the clearest representations of the effects of disobedience on the God and man relationship is found in the story of Adam and Eve in the Garden of Eden When man chose his desires over the directives of God. Yes, we can say that he was tempted, but a test only becomes a temptation when the tempter finds something inside us to work with. James explained man's cooperation with the enemy this way: *"Let no man say when he is tempted, I am tempted of God: for God cannot be tempted with evil, neither tempteth he any man: but every man is tempted, when he is drawn away of his own lust, and enticed. Then when lust hath conceived, it bringeth forth sin: and sin, when it is finished, bringeth forth death."* (James 1:13-15 KJV)

One old hymn puts it this way, *"Yield not to temptation, for yielding is sin. Each victory will help you, some others to win. Fight manfully onward, Dark passion subdue. Look ever to Jesus, He will carry you through."* **Horatio Richmond Palmer (1868)**. Our disobedience comes when we surrender our will to anything other than God. Many have said Adam didn't do a good job of stewardship as the head of his household, that he never taught Eve the value of obedience to God. Some have said that Adam had loved the creation more than the Creator. I'm not sure how true this is, and neither do I want to debate it here. What I know for sure is that this act of single disobedience changed how man related to God from then on. He was no longer communicating with God in the place of being robbed of the glory of God.

The great separation had taken place and there was now a breach in this flow of the divine and man. Yet, it didn't change how God related to man, no, it didn't and wouldn't, because there was the plan of redemption. The sinless lamb of God who was slain long before the foundation of the earth, will repair the breach of disobedience. This plan will re-establish the un-broken union between God and man, which He had created us for. The penalty for the effects of sin was paid in full when Jesus shed His blood for the remission of our sins.

"For the wages of sin is death, but the gift of God is eternal life through Jesus Christ our Lord." (Romans 6:23)

However, there's still the elephant in the room, that which separates us from God. It's the fact that we can use our free will to choose not to agree with God on any matter. Remember, Lucifer was the first to try this, and he still is and will always be paying the penalty for his disobedience. The justice of God, which is a product of His righteousness, demands a consequence for the disobedient soul. The Bible tells us that... *we say we love Him, but only when we are obedient do we really walk in love towards our God. (1 John 2:3-6 Paraphrased)* It also says, *"If you are willing and obedient, you shall eat the good of the land". Isa 1: 19-20)*

Therefore, the disobedient will receive their just rewards or consequences.1 John 3:4 CEV. Rebellion and doubt are some acts of disobedience that separates us from God because our love for Him is manifested in our obedience.

Takeaway

Your obedience to God is your love for Him in action.

Chapter 4
Our God Is a Faithful God

"The LORD, the Lord, a God merciful and gracious, slow to anger, and abounding in steadfast love and faithfulness." (Exodus 34:6 NLT)

*I*n the next two chapters or so we will examine some scriptural basis for our walking in obedience to God's spoken and written Word. Throughout the Bible, a lot is written about the nature and divine attributes of our Heavenly Father and yet we will never exhaust the topic. In this book, I have been given the task of focusing on His faithfulness and how we can experience it. God's faithfulness far surpasses our human understanding, yet God has decided to reveal it to us through our acts of loving obedience to Him.

Moses was the first person to whom God gave a practical display of His faithfulness. Exodus 34:4-9 (CEV) tells us, *"So, Moses cut two tablets of stone like the first. And he rose early in the morning and went up on Mount Sinai, as the LORD had commanded him, and took in his hand two tablets of stone. The LORD descended in the cloud and stood with him there and proclaimed the name of the LORD. The LORD passed before him and proclaimed, "The LORD, the LORD, a God merciful and gracious, slow to anger, and abounding in steadfast love and faithfulness, keeping steadfast love for thousands, forgiving iniquity and transgression and sin, but who will by no means clear the guilty, visiting the iniquity of the fathers on the children and the children's children, to the third and the fourth generation." And Moses quickly bowed his head toward the earth and worshiped".*

For us to have an idea of the degree of God's faithfulness let's look at the Hebrew meaning for faithful as used in the aforementioned scripture. This word is *Aman* (Awman), it speaks of-being permanent, true, certain, steadfast, sure, trusty, upholding, like a foster Father. This helps us to understand the trustworthiness of the God who has adopted us into divine sonship. Our adopted Father is sure, steadfast, morally true, and permanent in our lives as He daily sustains us. Our unfaithfulness will never lessen God's faithfulness.

The account of the prophet Jonah is an excellent example of the unwavering steadfastness of God.

"Now, the LORD had prepared (appointed, destined) a great fish to swallow Jonah. And Jonah was in the stomach of the fish three days and three nights." (Jon 1:17)

Among the many great Bible stories that I taught in various Sunday school classes, the story of Jonah ranks very high. Many times, when this story is taught, the impressionable young minds remember a man who was swallowed up by a big fish. Then, three days later the fish spat him back out on dry land. This story when recounted in a sermon or Bible study most times we find there's focus on the prophet's disobedience to the instructions of the Lord. I remember reading an article somewhere that said God allowed the fish to keep Jonah until he came to his senses and repented.

Looking at Jonah's story in hindsight, many well-minded Christians would say he got a very easy assignment, and had he been obedient at first, Nineveh could have been spared a lot of heartache and distress. Jonah's word was what allowed the inhabitants of Nineveh to experience the mercies of God. All Jonah had to do was to go and tell these people to turn from the wrong they were doing. Turn to God in repentance, and God will spare their lives. But Jonah almost lost his life for not wanting to obey this simple assignment. Jonah's disobedience was hinged on his emotions. He was a famous prophet, and when he brought the word that God was going to destroy the nation of Nineveh, the thought of God being merciful and sparing their lives was more than the renowned prophet could stand.

Therefore, dying at sea in a major storm he thought was a more reputable way to close the chapter of his life, but God who is faithful will always remain faithful would not allow Jonah to abort his purpose and destiny. There are times when the thing God instructs us to do is not favorable in our eyes or the eyes of others. Who knows, it might not be something good, it could be a difficult word, one of captivity and doom. The prophets of old have attested to that. Let's not forget Moses who was trying to convince God that he was not the best candidate for the job or the prophet Jeremiah who knew for sure that his obedience to God could cost him his life. Many of God's leaders and ministers have allowed pride and the opinion of men to cause them to commit spiritual abortion. The struggle between obedience to God and the pride of being accepted and liked by men has been an ongoing battle for some of God's dearly loved children. And unfortunately, oftentimes pride and men's views emerge victorious.

That huge fish that God sent right on time to catch Jonah as he came hurling from the side of the boat towards the water was God's faithfulness to the unfaithful prophet. God is altogether faithful whether or not we choose to be. This faithfulness is one of our Heavenly Father's moral attributes, the characteristics of God's divinity that are transferable to our humanity, so we as His children are able to be faithful as well. God is a God of second, or should I say many chances. He gave Jonah the privilege and opportunity to be found faithful to Him. True faithfulness is born from a place of trust, loyalty, and obedience. Trust, because we must firmly believe in the dependability and ability of God to do what He says He will do. Likewise, God must be assured of our reliability and ability to be obedient. Jonah's relationship with God was now being put to the test even more so than the heart of the people of Nineveh.

Being in the stomach of the fish for three days and three nights gave Jonah enough time to reposition his heart in obedience to the will of God.

Our Father in His omniscience knows us all by nature. He knows what we are capable of and desire to do. `He knows how to guide us to reposition our hearts to walk in faithfulness. God will help us despite our weaknesses; and in His goodness extends His faithfulness to us in spite of our disobedience. God has shown this through His beloved people in that every time the rebellious disobedient children of Israel repented of their sins; God showed them mercy. He never left them without a way to access Him and His grace. He outlined very early in their journey in the wilderness the importance of obedience and the blessings it brings. Deuteronomy 28 itemized the plan of God for obedience and disobedience. Let's refresh our minds or acquaint ourselves with the contents of this text.

"Now it shall come to pass, if you diligently obey the voice of the Lord your God, to observe carefully all His commandments which I command you today, that the Lord your God will set you high above all nations of the earth. And all these blessings shall come upon you and overtake you because you obey the voice of the Lord your God: "Blessed shall you be in the city, and blessed shall you be in the country.

"Blessed shall be the fruit of your body, the produce of your ground and the increase of your herds, the increase of your cattle and the offspring of your flocks. "Blessed shall be your basket and your kneading bowl. "Blessed shall you be when you come in, and blessed shall you be when you go out. "The Lord will cause your enemies who rise against you to be defeated before your face; they shall come out against you one way and flee before you seven ways. "The Lord will command the blessing on you in your storehouses and in all to which you set your hand, and He will bless you in the land which the Lord your God is giving you. "

The Lord will establish you as a holy people to Himself, just as He has sworn to you if you keep the commandments of the Lord your God and walk in His ways. Then all peoples of the earth shall see that you are called by the name of the Lord, and they shall be afraid of you. And the Lord will grant you plenty of goods, in the fruit of your body, in the increase of your livestock, and in the produce of your ground, in the land of which the Lord swore to your fathers to give you. The Lord will open to you His good treasure, the heavens, to give the rain to your land in its season, and to bless all the work of your hand. You shall lend to many nations, but you shall not borrow. And the Lord will make you the head and not the tail; you shall be above only, and not be beneath, if you heed the commandments of the Lord your God, which I command you today, and are careful to observe them. So, you shall not turn aside from any of the words which I command you this day, to the right or the left, to go after other gods to serve them. Deut 28:1-14 NKJV

I added the entire text concerning the blessings God has promised His people because our God is often portrayed as a hard, harsh God. So, I want to introduce you to Him as the kind, loving, faithful, and just God that He is. Let us not be in denial- He has decreed curses to fall upon the disobedient as well. Let's take a look at the remainder of Deuteronomy 28 chapter.

"But it shall come to pass if you do not obey the voice of the Lord your God, to observe carefully all His commandments and His statutes which I command you today, that all these curses will come upon you and overtake you: "Cursed shall you be in the city, and cursed shall you be in the country. "Cursed shall be your basket and your kneading bowl. "Cursed shall be the fruit of your body and the produce of your land,

the increase of your cattle and the offspring of your flocks. "Cursed shall you be when you come in, and cursed shall you be when you go out. "The Lord will send on you cursing, confusion, and rebuke in all that you set your hand to do until you are destroyed and until you perish quickly, because of the wickedness of your doings in which you have forsaken Me. The Lord will make the plague cling to you until He has consumed you from the land that you are going to possess. The Lord will strike you with consumption, with fever, with inflammation, with severe burning fever, with the sword, with scorching, and with mildew; they shall pursue you until you perish and your heavens which are over your head shall be bronze, and the earth which is under you shall be iron. The Lord will change the rain of your land to powder and dust; from the heaven, it shall come down on you until you are destroyed. "The Lord will cause you to be defeated before your enemies; you shall go out one way against them and flee seven ways before them; and you shall become troublesome to all the kingdoms of the earth. Your carcasses shall be food for all the birds of the air and the beasts of the earth, and no one shall frighten them away. The Lord will strike you with the boils of Egypt, with tumors, with the scab, and with the itch, from which you cannot be healed. The Lord will strike you with madness and blindness and confusion of heart. And you shall grope at noonday, as a blind man gropes in darkness; you shall not prosper in your ways; you shall be only oppressed and plundered continually, and no one shall save you. "You shall betroth a wife, but another man shall lie with her; you shall build a house, but you shall not dwell in it; you shall plant a vineyard but shall not gather its grapes. Your ox shall be slaughtered before your eyes, but you shall not eat of it; your donkey shall be violently taken away from before you and shall not be restored to you; your sheep shall be given to your enemies, and you shall have no one to rescue them. Your sons and your daughters shall be given to another people, and your eyes shall look and fail with longing for them all day long; and there shall be no strength in your hand. A nation whom you have not known shall eat the fruit of your land and the produce of your labor, and you shall be only oppressed and crushed continually. So you shall be driven mad because of the sight which your eyes see. The Lord will strike you in the knees and on the legs with severe boils which cannot be healed, and from the sole of your foot to the top of your head. "The Lord *will bring you and the king whom you set over you to a nation which neither you nor your fathers have known, and there you shall serve other gods—wood and stone. And you shall become an astonishment, a proverb, and a byword among all nations where the Lord will drive you. "You shall carry much seed out to the field but gather little in, for the locust shall consume it. You shall plant vineyards and tend them, but you shall neither drink of the wine nor gather the grapes; for the worms shall eat them. You shall have olive trees throughout all your territory, but you shall not anoint yourself with the oil; for your olives shall drop off. You shall beget sons and daughters, but they shall not be yours; for they shall go into captivity. Locusts shall consume all your trees and the produce of your land. "The alien who is among you shall rise higher and higher above you, and you shall come down lower and lower. He shall lend to you, but you shall not lend to him; he shall be the head, and you shall be the tail. "Moreover, all these curses shall come upon you and pursue and overtake you, until you are destroyed, because you did not obey the voice of the Lord your God, to keep His commandments and His statutes which He commanded you. (Deut 28:15-45 NKJV)*

My dear reader, God is faithful. He will faithfully give to us that which is our due portion. May I encourage you to get to know Him and I guarantee you that before long, obedience to Him and His word will be your joyful response.

Takeaway

Our disobedience does not negate God's faithfulness to bless us. It will only stop us from experiencing it.

Chapter 5
Our obedience to God is in proportion to our love for Him

Jesus said, "If ye love me, keep my commandments".
John 14:15 KJV

As we study God's Word, we realize that God requires a relationship with us that is based on our free will and loving obedience. A union that portrays the truth that both parties are poised to experience mutual benefits. Yet, there are many times when we, as the lovers of God, respond to His instructions in ways that are less than loving. We will use this section to briefly look at some of the ways we may respond to the instructions of God. Please bear in mind that this is by no means an established or exhaustive list. I'm simply saying that when the Word of God requires a response, the way we respond can be categorized in one or more of these forms.

Fearful Obedience

The first response can be called a response of fear. Before we can determine what fearful responses look like, let's look at an example of Moses and the children of Israel's relationship with God. As we have gathered from the account in the book of Exodus, Moses and the Israelites responses to God's instructions were poles apart. Moses' response to sensing the wooing of God was to draw near. His encounter with the burning bush is an illustration of this response.

Many people would run away or call someone else to go with them to inquire to see what was going on. But not Moses, he turned aside to go and find out why there was a fire, and the bush was not being consumed. My question to you is, what would you do? What your response is to any sensing of God will determine what your relationship with Him will be like. Will there be an increase or decrease in the communication flow?

God is always anticipating a response from us, and His Word reminds us that today when we hear His Word, we should not harden our hearts. From the text, we have been made aware that we have the ability to hear God's voice. Regardless of how we hear, whether we hear Him through the natural ear like the sounds around us or we hear Him within our spirits or we hear Him by the ear of the spirit. The Bible says that we can hear Him, and when we hear Him, there is an anticipated response. By simply turning aside, Moses became qualified to enter a personal intimate relationship with God, one that caused him to be chosen by God to lead His children Israel out of bondage. God knew that he had found in Moses one with an ear to hear the spirit and a heart that is willing to be close and obey His instructions.

Moses' relationship with the Lord and communication experiences grew steadily, and he became the means through whom God communicated the intent of His heart to Pharaoh for His children to be released from the bondage of slavery. Likewise, he spoke on God's behalf to His people Israel to tell them God's desires and instructions. Not only was Moses the go be-tween God and man, but he was meant to be the example to lead them into their own relationship with God. This he did with 70 Elders who joined him on the mountain to meet with the Lord. Though they might have been afraid like everyone else, their fear of God caused them to draw near to Him so they too could hear His instructions and obey.

The masses, on the other hand, had a different kind of fear. They were afraid of God, and this fear caused them to hide from Him. They literally stayed away from Him. So flesh-driven was their fear that on one occasion they all cried in unison; "Moses, you go up to the mountain and speak to God for us and then tell us what He wants us to do, and anything He tells us to do we will do it. Only don't let us have to draw near to Him. We will take second-hand instructions." And that's how it is with many of us today. We don't want to get too close to God. We want our pastors and church leaders to go and seek God and come and tell us what they think God is saying to us and for us. We will obey the instructions our pastors and leaders give us. We don't want to hear God for ourselves lest we be caught in the technicality of needing to obey. The fear many of us have for God greatly outweighs the love we have for Him. Here's a surprising reality, this unholy fear and separation can still produce a fruit of obedience, which might not be a loving obedience, but rather, a compulsive obedience for fear of the wrath of God, wrath they knew only too well from seeing what happened to the firstborn of the Egyptians. I cannot overemphasize the need to fear God, but this fear is not one birthed out of a phobia of a cruel regimental God. No! It's ascribing to Him reverential awe. This means to consciously give God the respect, honor, admiration, and worship that is due to Him.

Psalm 95 verses 6-9 calls us to demonstrate this fear: It says, *"Come and kneel before this Creator-God; come and bow before the mighty God, our majestic maker! For we are those He cares for, and He is the God we worship. Therefore, drop everything else and listen to His voice! For this is what he's saying:" Today when I speak, don't even think about turning a deaf ear to me like they did when they tested me at Meribah and Massah, the place where they argued with me, their Creator."* Psalm 95 verse 6-9 TPT.

Takeaway

When we come in contact with the Lord God Almighty, we'll be stirred into an innate supernatural awe of Him. This response will stimulate us into a place of honoring Him with loving obedience.

Willing Obedience

Unlike disciplined soldiers who by duty's call are bound to obey every command or order of their superior, our willingness to obey God is because we love Him. When we truly love God, we won't find His commandments burdensome. Neither will we respond to His instructions from the position of a fearful slave intimidated by the thought of punishment. No, our obedient response will be that of willing children responding to a loving Father whom we know and trust.

For this is the love of God, that we keep His commandments. And His commandments are not burdensome. 1John 5:3 NKJV

This is the ideal picture of what our willing obedience to God should be like, yet there are those of us who religiously read the Bible every day, holding on to its every promise, yet walking in disobedience to many of its relationship-building instructions. For instance, it is somewhat easier to obey the instruction to study the Word of God and many have given themselves to the discipline of daily studying the Word of God. But, somewhere in this exercise, we have yet to develop the mindset of doing what the Word requires. I guess this was what Dr. Luke was alluding to when he wrote, "*Jesus replied, "But even more blessed are all who hear the word of God and put it into practice." Luke 11:28 NLT.*

By willingly obeying God's Word, we will manifest new mindsets, with desires that are aligned with God's desires. And like Jesus, our will is now to do the will of our heavenly Father.

Partial obedience

In order to look at partial obedience, let's look at a story in the Bible that teaches us how easily we can suffer the penalty for disobedience, although we started in full obedience.

This is the story of two prophets in the book of 1 Kings chapter 13. At the beginning of the saga, God had given a young prophet from Judah an assignment to take a message to the king. He was also instructed not to stop and eat anything from those in the city to which God had sent him. God also told him to use a different route on his way home. The well-meaning young man of God did what the Lord told him to do.

He went to Bethel to the king, delivered the message, and was en route via another way, heading back home. He stopped and rested but little did he realize that he was being positioned for the test of true obedience. This test was broken into two segments:

1. To carry out the assignment of delivering the word.

2. To get back home safely.

As the story progressed, we were told that there was another prophet living in Bethel, whom the author of 1 Kings described as an old prophet. When this old prophet heard that the young prophet had gone to the king and delivered a message from God to him, he made it his business to seek out this young man of God. The old prophet told the young man of God that he had a word from God for him and encouraged him to have a meal with him. A word which turned out to be contrary to the instruction that he had received from God.

There was no mention of the young prophet seeking God to see if there was a change of plans. He switched his obedience to align himself with the instructions from the old prophet. This lie of the old prophet led to the demise of the young prophet. Let's look at how a word from the wrong source can take us on the path of disobedience. The story of the prophets' encounter went this way.

"And went after the man of God, and found him sitting under an oak: and he said unto him, Art thou the man of God that camest from Judah? And he said, I am. Then he said unto him, come home with me, and eat bread. And he said, I may not return with thee, nor go in with thee: neither will I eat bread nor drink water with thee in this place: For it was said to me by the word of the Lord, thou shalt eat no bread nor drink water there, nor turn again to go by the way that thou camest. He said unto him, I am a prophet also as thou art; and an angel spake unto me by the word of the LORD, saying, bring him back with thee into thine house, that he may eat bread and drink water. But he lied unto him. So, he went back with him and did eat bread in his house and drank water. And it came to pass, as they sat at the table, that the word of the LORD came unto the prophet that brought him back: And he cried unto the man of God that came from Judah, saying, Thus saith the

LORD, Forasmuch, as thou hast, disobeyed the mouth of the LORD, and hast not kept the commandment which the LORD thy God commanded thee, But camest back, and hast eaten bread and drunk water in the place, of the which the Lord did say to thee, eat no bread, and drink no water; thy carcass shall not come unto the sepulcher of thy fathers. "And it came to pass, after he had eaten bread, and after he had drunk, that he saddled for him the ass, to wit, for the prophet whom he had brought back. And when he was gone, a lion met him by the way, and slew him: and his carcass was cast in the way, and the ass stood by it, the lion also stood by the carcass. And behold, men passed by, and saw the carcass cast in the way, and the lion standing by the carcass: and they came and told it in the city where the old prophet dwelt. And when the prophet that brought him back from the way heard thereof, he said, it is the man of God, who was disobedient unto the word of the LORD: therefore, the LORD hath delivered him unto the lion, which hath torn him, and slain him, according to the word of the LORD, which he spake unto him.

In some of the previous chapters, we realized that Bethel had fallen into a state of spiritual decline, hence the need for God to dispatch a prophet with a message for its King. The citizens of this country were living in disobedience to God. The people were living in idolatry worshipping a golden calf, just as their ancestors had done in the wilderness. Maybe this could be a reason for the old prophet delivering a word of untruth to the young prophet. Who knows whether or not the old prophet was living in a place of spiritual compromise? Spiritual compromise is a subtle form of disobedience that ends in decline.

So, although the young prophet had a connection with God and could intercede for the king's healing and was heard by God, he had the responsibility to obey God fully, even while sojourning in a place of idolatry.

Takeaway

We must obey what God tells us to do. Always check in with Him concerning any change of plans.

Loving Obedience

In the scriptures, we are exhorted to love the Lord our God with our entire being. A love of this nature will lead to us becoming bondservants of the living God. Love is an action word that requires us to display what we are experiencing. Therefore, a walk of loving obedience to God will cause us to display some of the following characteristics.

Having a genuine love for God.

We know from some of the passages written by John the beloved of God that there is a connection between loving God and obeying Him.

"He who hears My commandments and keeps them is the one who loves Me." John 14:21

He who says, "I know Him," and does not keep His commandments, is a liar, and the truth is not in him. But whoever keeps His word, truly the love of God is perfected in him. By this we know that we are in Him. (1 John 2:3-5 NKJV)

These are only two texts that clearly show that loving the Almighty God and obeying Him are intertwined.

Bearing the mark of true discipleship

A disciple is a disciplined one. Our loving obedience to God will cause us to display a surrendered and submissive heart in response to the Holy Spirit's instructions or commands.

Like soldiers in an army who follow their chain of command's orders without flinching and procrastinating, this becomes the hallmark of a true servant of God.

Manifesting genuine Fruit of the Spirit

Jesus said in John chapter 15 that our bearing of genuine spiritual fruit is a result of us being attached to Him. The vine from the tree of life, i.e., Jesus in state of being, therefore, our loving obedience will bring us into a God-initiated reattachment (engraftment) to the "true vine" (Verse 1) without whom we cannot produce fruit that will remain (Verse 16).

"Abide in Me, and I in you. As the branch cannot bear fruit of itself unless it abides in the vine, neither can you, unless you abide in Me. "I am the vine; you are the branches. He who abides in Me, and I in him, bears much fruit; for with-

out Me, you can do nothing. If anyone does not abide in Me, he is cast out as a branch and is withered; and they gather them and throw them into the fire, and they are burned". John15:1-6)

Loving obedience will bring us into that divine attachment to Jesus which brings the life-bearing fruit of the Spirit.

Having a committed prayer life

Our ability to hear the voice of God is the product of time spent with Him. Like every relationship, the more time people spend in each other's company, the closer their union becomes. It is in such times of intimacy that secret matters are discussed, and commitments made. When individuals share habitable space, they not only know each other's voices but their ways and attitudes as well.

Moses and David are two men who displayed knowledge of the person of God. Moses, in his humbled state of friendship with God on various occasions, bargained with Him for the souls of men. David, when he wronged God by numbering the Israelites laid the lives of both the entire nation and himself at the mercies of God. This he did because He knew God's heart towards Israel. Both men from their prayer lives could stand in the counsel of God on behalf of disobedient men.

Let us strive to establish and maintain an unbroken prayer life where we can grow to know and obey God more.

Dwelling in a place of divine peace

The more we know God, the greater will be our trust and dependency upon Him. As we lovingly obey His will for our lives while carrying out His divine instruction toward others, we will experience a morphing into a more Christ-like attitude through which we will reveal the Prince of Peace to a world of turmoil and war where we must display and communicate God's love.

God's love language is obedience

God already displayed His love for us, by giving His only begotten son to die for our sins. All He requires in return is our loving Him in return. "*If you love Me, keep My commandments*". *(John 14:15)* For us to get a glimpse of God's love for us we can look at Philippians 2:5-8.

This is one of my favorite scriptures. Here, Paul counsels the church in Philippi to, *"Let this mind be in you which was also in Christ Jesus, who, being in the form of God, did not consider it robbery to be equal with God, but made Himself of no reputation, taking the form of a bondservant, and coming in the likeness of men. And being found in appearance as a man, He humbled Himself and became obedient to the point of death, even the death of the cross." (Phil 2:5-8 NKJV)*

Therefore, any true love for God will lead to dying to self and becoming an obedient servant. Now we can see that obeying God is one way of getting closer to Him and that absolute obedience can be equated to a genuine life abandoned to the worship of God. In some of the remaining chapters of this book, I have shared a few of my responses to God's call to loving obedience.

Chapter 6
Obedience When It Doesn't Make Sense

*O*beying God whether or not we understand what He is doing will bring forth His faithfulness. "To *those who are faithful, He shows Himself faithful". (Psalm 18:25).* Being faithful to God requires continuous obedience to His leading. When I first arrived in America, my sister who is my senior pastor, told me that the Lord wanted me to be ordained as an evangelist. No sooner than she spoke the word my answer was "No". Unequivocally no. When you have been exposed to 'churchianity' (all church and no relationship), like I had been, it's easy to have a weird perception of the various offices of the church. An evangelist for me was an elderly lady dressed in a big white hat wearing full white from head to toe, speaking in tongues continually. At age 42, I was not going to morph into that picture in my mind. My pastor told me to go pray about it. Honestly, I never wanted to pray because I had a feeling she was right. I felt that stirring in my spirit when she spoke those words. Note to self here, " Do not ask God to do something you don't want to experience." Some years ago, in a casual conversation with the Lord, I told Him to speak loudly because I might be spiritually hard of hearing. O, how He answered that prayer. Again, I was pulling another Jonah stunt, going the other way. I was on my way to work after the conversation with my sister and while on the bus, a sister engaged me in a conversation about the Lord. We were enjoying our conversation with soft intermittent hallelujahs when I was interrupted by a woman sitting across from us. She looked at me and asked, "What is your calling?" I replied, "I teach Sunday school, I am the Director of the Youth Ministry." But before I could finish my repertoire of church activities, she said, "I didn't ask you what you did". She spoke with her loudest, strongest voice, "God says to tell you, you are an evangelist." Thanks be to God the next stop was mine. I quickly ran off that bus to the stop for my connecting bus. While waiting, I said to the Lord, "Why did she have to tell the whole bus?" He responded, "You said you were hard of hearing." I called my pastor and told her what had happened. Her response was, "Well, I guess we have to schedule an ordination service pretty soon." The whole chain of events was an outworking of an evangelist mantle, which was given to me some years prior. Again, I can't over-emphasize that obedience is the key to unlocking God's faithfulness.

A lot of the things I am experiencing now started in Jamaica but were made to be manifested in America. I must make it known; that I never had an American dream. I thought I would be the one to turn the lights out if everyone was jumping off the Jamaica ship. The mantle of the Evangelist was given to me in Jamaica, but ordination came in America. Sometimes we experience God's faithfulness on other shores.

Always be open to change of location. *This is the story of how I got the mantle of the Evangelist.*

I cannot recall the exact year, but it was a season in which a very popular evangelist was having crusades all over the island. He was a favorite of the members of my church, so they turned out in their numbers to support him. Sometimes I can be an enigma. I told my friends that I was not rushing to go to the crusade. A whole week had passed before I said to them, "Let's go check out what is going on there." We went the Monday night, and the title of his message was, "Mantle night is my night for my thing from my God." The preacher said God had told him that on Friday night, he should pass his mantle on to someone. Now, this man's mantle was a pair of white shoes. It looked to me like about a male size 13, but I could be wrong. In the middle of his message, he prophesied about a lady who said she was not following up the crusade and had only come tonight to see what was going on. My friends were in awe and turned and said to me, "that's you he's speaking about." I laughed and said in my heart let's see what else he had to say. He then said, "God says to tell you He has set you up- again" in one of those so loud you can't miss it voice.

My friends ran to the altar and touched his shoes. I said there was no way I was going to touch his shoes, he's not Jesus.

There was an altar call and the night ended. It was then I was apprehended by the Holy Spirit. I mean an apprehension that had me physically stuck in one place. I could hear my friends asking for me and although I kept shouting "here I am," no one could hear me. I cried out to the Lord and said, "What is this?" He then told me to go and tell the preacher that He said that mantle night was my night. It was hard to see the Evangelist after he finished preaching, I pulled some family strings and he decided to speak with me. When I told him what the Lord told me, he held his stomach and laughed at me. He said what if everyone told him the same thing. It's only one mantle. I was deeply embarrassed and asked the Lord what I had done to receive that insult. I cried, I whined, and complained to God the entire time.

When I got into the car with my friends and told them what happened, one tried to encourage me by saying, "God chooses whomever He wants to, and I should be careful not to offend God." Sure enough, I think I did. It was one of the times I can recall feeling the displeasure I was giving my God. In that moment I realized how my pride had placed a wedge in our relationship. In short, I was telling God, yes! I will do this, but only on my terms. I felt the awe of God coming upon me as I shuddered at the thought of not being in a place of communing with the way I had grown to know. When I got out of the car, I fell flat on the driveway leading to my house. They had to take me up and carry me into my bedroom. I laid prostrate before the Lord in repentance, and He told me to go on a fast. He told me not to go back until Friday night after I had sanctified myself, which I did. Friday night when I was getting dressed, I heard the Holy Spirit say, "If I were you, I would wear a pair of pants." I said to Him, "Do you want me to lose my membership? You know we are not allowed to wear pants to services," but I obeyed. I am so glad I was obedient.

I arrived at the meeting very late, the praise and worship had just ended, and the preacher was about to begin. There was much hype and I never heard much of his message as the weight of the anointing was upon me. I was having my own Acts 2 moment feeling very drunk under the anointing. He preached and then made the altar call. He emphasized that the mantle had to be passed on that night. I remained in my seat during all of this. Then the Holy Spirit invited me to go to the altar. They had laid linoleum on the ground. The Holy Spirit said, "Go stand on the linoleum and watch what I will do." At that point I wasted no time, I quickly headed for the front of the altar. The moment I stepped on the linoleum, the preacher told everyone who was praising and worshipping with their hands raised to take them all down. Then he started to prophesy and said, "There is a woman here in the midst that God wants to get the mantle." He kept pacing the rostrum until he discerned where I was. He was surprised to see that it was me. He yelled out in Jamaican vernacular "Ah yuh?" meaning, "Oh it's you." He then asked one of his team members to remove my shoes and put his on my feet. I fell so many times under the weightiness of the anointing. I thank God I obeyed His suggestion and wore the pants.

I must let you know that I had forgotten about this entire event, until around the time of my ordination. That was when everything started coming back to my memory. I must testify that when we fully obey the Lord, we will encounter great measures of His faithfulness in ourselves.

Chapter 7
Obedience Will Cause Us to Walk Into Our Destiny

If you are willing and obedient, you will eat the good of the land. (Isaiah 1:19).

Many people have read this popular passage of scripture but might not have given it enough thought. In this passage is a key that guarantees God's people a life in which the providential power of God will constantly be available to us. Taking a closer look at this scripture we will see that the benefits of eating the goods of the land are conditional. When the word "if" is at the beginning of the verse it indicates that there is an option. We get to choose whether or not we want to be willing and obedient. Believe it or not, at the crux of our walk with the Lord is the requirement for us to use our free will to walk in obedience to Him. Obedience to God is the hallmark of true faith in Him. It puts our love for Him on display for the world to see.

Years ago, the Lord instructed me to go to Bible School. It was a regular Sunday morning service in

54

which I responded to an altar call. At the altar, I stood with two of my friends as the visiting speaker prophesied over us. He said that God had called us to go to Bible School, to be trained for what He has called us to do. We all received the word and said yes, we would. However, my friends ran with the word, and it wasn't long before they were both in different Bible schools. Two years had passed, and I was still not attending Bible School. Frankly speaking, I never felt any prodding nor an unction. I just kept it in the back of my mind that I needed to go to Bible School. Occasionally, I would enquire of God about schools that I heard about and waited for His responses. I must confess some of His answers were strange, for want of a more suitable adjective. Two of these answers I remember very clearly. I asked about a very prominent seminary, and like Samuel looking at Eliab (King David's eldest brother), I said to myself, surely, this is the place the Lord has chosen- (Samuel 16: 6-13 paraphrased for expression) I saw this place as the ideal place to study, to get deep into the Word of God. However, His response was that you would graduate from there with excellence and a lot of head knowledge but no relationship with Me. My response was "You are what I want, Lord."

The next was another renowned institution, His answer to this was very graphic. He said, "They do not know how to pack a fruit basket. They will put the melons on top of the bananas." I chuckled as I pictured the bananas being squashed to nothing. Notwithstanding, destroying the fruit that a believer bears is no laughing matter. So, I said to myself, I might just be bringing forth bananas, so again I patiently waited for His prodding to guide me to the right place.

My friends had become very concerned about my delay and kept pointing me in the direction of several Bible institutions. But, during my waiting period, God revealed something more about His plan for me. Not only was I to go to school, but I was a valedictorian. This was where things got rocky, and the mindset of Jonah came to the forefront again. My head was in another direction, my mind shouted because I am an ambivert, that sweet mixture of introversion and extroversion. Talking my family and friends' ears off is an easy feat, but giving a valedictory speech was a totally different matter. Although I had maintained excellent grades in school, another of my best-kept secrets, the thought of being the person who would stand before everyone to give the brainiac speech was not something I was looking forward to doing.

This needed special grace from God. Yet, I surrendered to His plan while hoping it was my mind.

By now, many of the brethren in the church thought I was either walking in total disobedience or had missed out on God's timing. Not so! because it wasn't long before I again heard that familiar voice of the Lord speaking through me, telling a friend of mine that I was going to give our Pastor a Bible School application form to sign. She was ecstatic and started to ask me a barrage of questions. I had to quiet her, because like herself I was hearing this plan of God for the very first time.

The Lord told me to attend The Whole Life Ministries Bible School which was a part of the Fellowship Tabernacle Ministry with Pastor Al Miller as its President. This was the first time I heard of this school. I inquired of my brother who knew Pastor Miller if he had such an institution. At the time he was not sure, so together we checked it out and collected my application form. When my Pastor got the form to sign, he asked me why I wasn't going to the school that is associated with my church body. I so wanted to say, "Sir, God said they don't know how to pack a fruit basket", but with the humblest way I knew to respond, I said, "Sir, I am following the Lord's leading."

My Pastor's question led me to inquire of God why this school was His choice for me. He said, "I am leading you into practical ministry". I received that answer with gladness because I always told others that I am more of a practical than a theoretical person.

I just want to stop here and tell you how much I love the Lord. I love Him because He first loved me. No seriously, He loves me. His plans for me are good and not for disaster, to give me a future and hope. (Jeremiah 29:11. New Living Translation paraphrased). I am a practical person, I majored in Building Construction in High school although I failed miserably in my final year. (this might be for another book at another time). I started classes at the Whole Life Ministries Bible School in the September semester, and I was never, ever the same. During my first week of classes the Spirit of the Lord said to me, "You are going to fail your first test". I quickly replied, "Who fails in Bible school?" I said, "God I don't normally fail at anything in school, why would Bible School be any different?" Again, God said, "You are going to fail your first test." My dear reader please note this was a "verily, verily" moment. When something is said twice in the Bible without a doubt it will surely happen, and it did. This was not before I gave God a proposal, "If I fail my first test, then I will come to you on my knees and seek Your face to find out what is it that You require of me".

Our first test was for us to write a paper on worship at the end of the teachings on Praise and Worship. Yes! I said to myself, "Who fails praise and worship? Every Christian knows how to praise and worship God, so by my standards I wrote an excellent piece. But God is not a man that He should lie. I failed my first test. The passing grade was 75% and I got 73%. Not only did I fail the test and must redo it, but the teacher let me know my handwriting was illegible. That's something I have never heard before because many people have told me that they like my penmanship, so I know this was God breaking me. I redid my test and failed it again with the teacher complaining he had no idea what I was trying to say. This was the straw that broke the camel's back.

I rushed home that evening and went straight on my knees beside my bed. I asked the Lord what He was trying to tell me. What does He want me to do? His response was quick, He said, "You will do it my way. I took you to Bible School and I'm going to keep you there. You must submit to my leading and walk in obedience because you are a valedictorian." I wept! Not because I had a problem walking with the Lord in obedience, but because I could feel His loving harness being placed over me. I knew for sure that He was calling me to accept the invitation to walk with Him step by step during this season. I said yes. We did my test, and I got a 98 on it.

My encounter with that teacher did not end there because the Lord gave me a dream about him and told me to tell him what the Lord was saying. He wept when he got the word from the Lord. He knew that his season at the institution had ended and left at the end of the month to pursue other areas of ministry.

Do you recall I said that the Lord chose that school for me because He wanted me to learn practical Ministry? Well, the school had a particular program that was called "Practical Ministry". For this course, students had to go out and volunteer in different facilities. I was stationed at a Salvation Army home and a place of safety for boys. God used those time of volunteering to develop within me discernment, wisdom, and understanding all wrapped up in love.

Before long the year ended, and I was not the valedictorian. I said to myself, "I don't think God had said that; that was definitely my pride." Right there, even though I said I didn't want to be someone who would give a speech I chided myself for being so presumptuous. At the end of our graduation exercise, I felt complete and that I had done what the Lord wanted me to do. I was ready to move on.

The Bible lets us know- that many are the plans of a man's heart but only the plans of God will come to pass. - He was not done with me. He used a fellow student to tell me that He wanted me to be back in school the next school year. I chuckled and said, "God never told me that." He said, "Well He told me to tell you that."

I laughed and bade him farewell and went about my business. I had great plans for my summer break, I was going to America to see my sisters and shop. The Lord allowed me to do that, but He was not through with me. On my way home while on the plane, the Lord said to me, "You need to return to Bible School, I'm not through with you". My response was "Yes Lord", and my thought was I would save some money and register to attend classes in the January semester.

When I arrived home, I went to visit my friend and told her what the Lord had said. She laughed, and said, "God has a big plan for you, He's not done yet." I agreed and said I would register for classes in the New Year. Then I heard myself saying to her, "I have to be at the school on Tuesday evening. I must be in class again, she laughed and said, "I thought you said you were going in for January." So, I stopped her and said, "I'm hearing this again for the first time, but God wants me to be there."

I went to the school the next Tuesday, registered, and went straight to the class because I had used up all my money on my vacation, I had to enter into an installment plan to pay my tuition, but I know how in God's eyes obedience is better than sacrifice (See Samuel)

God did some remarkable things during that year at school. Many classes were rescheduled resulting in a lot of shifting. Subsequently, some of the classes I took in that year I was supposed to have taken in the fourth year of school. God will shift everything to suit His plan for our lives. While in school the Lord kept speaking to me about migrating to the USA. and being beside my sister in ministry. He said, "I have trained you for this." I was so focused on the Lord that I did not realize that the course I was doing would lead to being an ordained minister, honestly, I had never inquired about the course curriculum, I went because God told me to go. Regarding migrating to the USA, His instruction to me took the form of a riddle. He said,

"June is too soon, but July you could try, but by August you must."

I dragged for as long as I could but as I previously said, I took the last flight out of Jamaica on the last day of August 2023.

To encourage my heart the Lord came telling me things along the way that would happen when I get to America. He made provisions for me. The last time I was with my sisters she was living in a small bedroom that the church was paying for. I came to America prepared to sleep on the floor beside her bed. I wanted to know what God had in mind and I wasn't going to miss it for anything, bed, or no bed.

God did not fail at His faithfulness. Upon my arrival, God had relocated her into a beautiful furnished one-bedroom apartment with more than enough space for both of us. I was also registered in seminary. This my dear reader was one of the main reasons God chose that Bible school for me; I could easily transfer the credits from it to my new institution. Praise be to God! His ways are past finding out.

I transitioned smoothly into the advanced class and was granted a scholarship. I was the class president and honor student that year, all by God's grace. The following year I was in the bachelor's group and graduated top of the class. My obedience to migrate to New York caused me to see where God had established me as the valedictorian. All God requires is our walk in loving obedience for us to encounter His faithfulness.

Valedictorian Day

While preparing for the big day, I asked my Heavenly Father what I should say. He told me to tell them that I said, "Obedience is the Key to unlocking my faithfulness." I did what He said. Many people came to me after and said they felt the unction to attend the seminary and that they now realized it was attainable.

Sometime later I reached out to my classmates from the other Bible School to share my testimony, only to realize that from that group I was the only person still in Bible school. The entire batch was scrapped for various reasons the year I migrated. God's plan didn't stop there. He took me all the way to the Doctorate level of studies. The day I graduated with my Doctorate, I could picture my Heavenly Father laughing, because eight years earlier I told one of my friends who was at the altar with me, "God would not keep me in Bible school so long, it's not as if I am going to become a medical Dr. I am too old for all that studying." Again, let me reiterate that all the honor and glory belong to Him and Him alone.

Chapter 8
Obedience Will Bring God Glory (Part1)

*M*any time as believers, we live from that place of carnality. We process what we hear in our hearts from a place of what we conceive or perceive in our minds and not from what we know to be true about God. That's why many good, intended children of God are yet to walk in loving obedience to God. The Bible lets us know that the same God who sits high and looks down low (Psalm138:6), that very same God is Jehovah Jireh. There is nowhere in the Bible that says He only provides houses, jobs, and cars. It did say that He supplies all our needs according to His riches in glory through Christ Jesus our Lord. (Phil 4:29) And that He is faithful. (Deut 7:9)

Another one of the awesome things about God is that He does not deal with us according to the way we deal with Him. *"If we are not faithful, he will still be faithful. Christ cannot deny who he is." (2 Timothy 2:13 CEV).* In His mercy He allowed me to get my opportunity to be on the other end of a story similar to the one I shared at the beginning of the book.

While I was still living in Jamaica the Lord called me into a time of shut-in. I was in my house for a week and totally forgot to go grocery shopping before starting my fast. Everything went well during my time of fasting but when I got to Sunday, I went straight to church without having my beloved breakfast. I said, "Lord, when I am off this fast, I would really love to have some eggs and sausage: I guess you figured it out by now the eggs and sausage were my go-to breakfast. But there wasn't any in the house because my son had consumed what was there. Realizing my situation, I lifted my eyes to heaven and asked the Lord very casually, "God I wish someone would give me two eggs and a can of sausage I would make a "mean" breakfast first thing tomorrow." So, as a sister for my church would say, "I prayed and put it down". I had a Sunday evening service to attend. I left the house and headed for church.

I was walking quickly towards the sanctuary trying to catch my favorite seat when my girlfriend called me. She was trying to get my attention for one of the seniors from the church who wanted to speak with me. The sister who wanted to speak with was someone I dearly loved. I will never forget her. She was very elderly and pretty much kept to herself. But she always had God's attention and so she had mine. We were very good friends.

I just loved the way she loved the Lord. Sister Harvey was her name. I mentioned her by name because I wanted to honor her. She was a strong praying woman who was very jovial and kind in spirit. I turned around in response to her call and I saw her waving a plastic bag at me. When I got closer to her it was a used bread bag. Those plastic bags that you can see right through it. Inside the bag were two brown eggs (my favorite kind) and a can of Vienna sausage.

I hugged her, squeezed her, and said, "Thank you so much for having the "ear of a spirit. See Rev, I knew it was my Father who told you to give this to me." She smiled and said, "God said to give you this". I was deeply moved by what she did for some of these reasons:

1   Her ability to hear God so precisely.
2   Her willing obedience.
3   I knew it was a sacrifice because she never had a lot of money. And finally, how compassionate she was.

I thanked her deeply and gave God the glory. Here no flesh was glorified in His presence. My dear sister's obedience caused me to experience a taste of God's faithfulness. I thanked God for hearing a simple prayer. To think that so many deep intercessions were happening on the same frequency as my sigh of prayer, yet He responded to it. I thanked Him also for His speedy and loving response. That my dear reader was yet another one of my life-transforming moments. I felt like a dearly loved child sitting on my daddy's knees.

The God that we serve is a personal and dear friend and a good father who loves us in spite of us.

Chapter 9
God's Light Shines Through Those Who Are Obedient

*W*hile still in my first year of Bible School in Jamaica, the Lord was continually giving me instructions that required my obedience even when it did not line up with what was happening in school.

One such instance was when we were required to write a 2-minute talk paper. I wrote a paper about being an evangelist simply by carrying the presence of the Lord. I used the example of someone traveling on the bus and causing the person that sat beside them to be drawn to the Lord just by carrying His presence and releasing it when He wanted to be released.

God's test of my obedience came when He told me to speak on the night I was not rostered to speak. The spirit of the Lord told me to take my paper with me and to be ready to speak. I was definitely not jumping but I obeyed. As the evening progressed a few people presented their papers while others were saying that they weren't ready. The president then asked if there was anyone here who wasn't supposed to speak but had their paper with them. I sheepishly raised my hand and made my way to the front as he said come. I started to read while being conscious of the time, but then the spirit of the Lord decided that He wanted to use me for His glory. I remember hearing someone saying her 2 minutes are up, and the president saying, "Do not stop her, let her continue." My recollection of that moment was me expressing what it would be like if we carried the presence of the Lord wherever we went. Everyone could experience Him in the way He desired to be experienced. Looking back, I can see that it was God's will to give us a practical example of how He wanted us to be. Even writing it now, I'm still humbled and moved to tears at the thought that the King of Glory, the Teacher of teachers, would use me to express His heart to my fellow students.

There was yet another instance when the Lord used me in a similar way during that first year in school. I will tell you this, "obedience is truly the key to unlocking God's faithfulness." A practice of most Bible Schools is that the students go on campaigns for the school. We would volunteer or be asked to minister in different areas according to our calling and preferences. I had volunteered to teach a Sunday school class at an Outreach Church because that was my role in my church. However, about two weeks before this event, I was sitting in a class when the Lord gave me a message coming from the Book of Ruth. It was a very practical message about how we should treat others who are in our care as believers. I wrote the message during a class as the Holy Spirit overshadowed me to do it. I kept this close to my heart. I didn't know why the Lord wanted that message. However, in true form, when Sunday morning came for us to gather together and be transported to the churches that we were assigned, the Lord said, "Take the message with you." After assembly and prayer, the Dean of the school asked, "Is there anyone here who we had not assigned to preach, but God gave you a message?" Again, I sheepishly raised my hand, trembling like a leaf, and said, "Yes He did." She smiled and said to me, "Oh it's you", I wasn't sure what that meant.

I was sent to the largest church and given the awesome task of bringing forth the message God had given to me. God proved faithful again as He took pleasure in my obedience. He delivered and blessed His people. Trusting God to faithfully honor His word is fundamental to walking in obedience.

Chapter 10
Godly Obedience
Will Open Doors for Miracles

*W*hen it was time for Jesus to manifest the first miracle on earth, His mother Mary instructed the servers to follow any instructions Jesus gave them. This one act of obedience brought forth the revelation of the authority and power that the man Jesus was walking in. (John 2) The key here is obedience even when it seems like it's a "This is it"? moment.

What would you do?

Do you have the faith to move containers of water around not knowing what the water can be changed to? The scripture tells us that in jars of clay are hidden divine treasures. That the excellency might be of God and not us. (2 Corinthians 4:7-9) You and I are simply jars of clays carrying the water of the Holy Spirit within our beings. Our obedience is fundamental to miracles being wrought on the earth. One obedient vessel filled with the water of God's Holy Spirit can permeate an entire gathering with the outpouring of miracles, deliverance, and breakthroughs. One morning I was waiting at a bus stop for a connecting bus. While standing there the familiar voice of the Lord unctioned me to sing a worship song. All I heard was "Sing me a love song." I have learned that obeying this voice will cause me to walk in sync with some plan that God has on His heart. Again, I wasn't sure what to expect nor did I know His plan, but I started to sing. "I love You Lord and I lift my voice to worship You. Oh, my soul rejoice..." As I sang softly and swayed, He said, "Sing louder". This I quickly did because I was standing at the side of the shed away from others. I guess God was now testing my love for Him.

I sang louder until I was caught up in the worship that came from the song's anointing. Unknown to me, God was using the song to capture the attention of a lady standing close by. When the bus arrived and as I was boarding it the lady tapped me on the shoulder and remarked how clean I was. At first, I had no idea what that meant, but her second statement brought clarity. She asked me if I could pray for her and I said, "Yes." When I got to my seat, I said to God, "Holy Spirit please remind me, because You know I will forget." I was led to pray right there and then. While praying in the spirit I heard do not pray for her pray with her. I looked around just in time to see her alighting from the bus. I ran through the front door and yelled at her. "My sister, my sister God wants me to pray with you, not for you." She was very grateful and as we prayed together, the Holy Spirit delivered a word of knowledge telling her that the prayer request that she made for the person who lived in the building across the street from where we were standing, that God has bought the answer now. We were both apprehended by the power of God that she started to fall out right there on the pavement. I caught her and we stepped to the side. God told her she was to go upstairs and lay hands on the person and declare healing. That was when she explained that her sister lived in the building across the street and that she was battling cancer. I encouraged her and said, "Well her healing is in your hand." She ran across the street filled with joy and eager anticipation. One of the Pastors from my church always says, "Anticipation brings manifestation." Praise be to God! for faithfully respon-ding to my sister's prayers.

Obeying for my Miracle

Several years had passed and now I was the one in need of a miracle. It was in the evening, and we had returned home from church, everyone was relaxed and resting in their rooms when I remembered something. I went to see my sister in her room and spoke with her a bit. I left her room and headed downstairs to grab a snack, but as I was descending, I slipped on the last step and fell flat on my butt. There was an excruciating pain coming from my right knee area and when I raised myself up to look, I saw my leg dangling from my knee. I called out to my sisters and told them to bring the anointing oil and a cup of communion. I know this sounds like an odd thing to ask for, but some years prior to this, I had a vision of someone lying down at the foot of our stairs. The person looked dead. When I saw the formation of my body on the ground, I realized the vision I'd been seeing all these years turned out to be what I was experiencing, so I wasn't taking any chances.

I prayed for my health, anointed myself, and partook in the communion. By now my sisters wanted to lift me, but I told them not to because of how my knee was positioned. I dragged myself and made it to the sofa. We sent for help, and I was taken to the ER. Upon arriving at the ER, I was diagnosed with a ruptured quad tendon muscle that needed surgery. Unfortunately, there wasn't any orthopedic surgeon present. The doctor at the ER told me that I had to have the surgery no later than Friday because the muscle would have shrunk so badly, that it would have affected the way I walked in the future. Finding an orthopedic surgeon that fits into my insurance group was much easier said than done. It wasn't until late Monday afternoon that someone referred me to a surgeon who had done surgery on her husband some years prior.

Although he was not in my insurance group, he was more than willing to take a look at me. He recommended that I return to the ER on a Wednesday, and he would meet me there. Agreeing with him on this, I went into one of my short talks with God. I said to my heavenly Father, "I know you're the miracle-working God, if you're still going to do a miracle, I think I'm a great candidate Father." I placed my hand on my knee and believed God for His hand to touch me. There was no warmth running up my leg, and there was no shivering up my spine but somehow, He touched it. Somehow His miraculous touch met my faith right at my point of need. I did my due diligence concerning the doctor that I was going to see on Wednesday.

I read an article about another doctor with the same name who was also an orthopedic surgeon but was killed at point-blank range in a meeting. My heart was touched by the story, and I immediately assumed that it was this kind doctor's father. I started to pray for him, but I had no idea he too was going to be in line for a miracle as well.

We met in the ER and when he looked at me and saw the way I was positioned on the bed, he asked, "Can you raise your leg?" I said, "Yes", so he said, "Raise it let me see." To my surprise and his, my leg was elevated way above my spine. He looked at me in shock and said, "You're not supposed to be able to do that based on what I have seen in your image reports, you're not supposed to be able to do that." He said, "I have to do another screening on you to see what's going on."

We scheduled another CT scan for that afternoon and when the results came, he said, "It looks like you're being healed, your muscle is healing itself, mending itself." I started to testify to him about God when the Holy Spirit told me to tell him I had a message for him from God but I'm not to give it to him then. I asked him if he believed in God, and he said "yes" and that he was of the Catholic faith. I said, "great." He then told me that there wasn't anything more the hospital could do for me. I was to lay in the brace for a couple of weeks and just allow it to complete what it had already started to do. When God is at work, things go beyond the normal. The doctor then said to me, I will come and visit you at home just to see how you're progressing because there won't be a need for you to come to the hospital again for this. I prayed with him a bit. As promised, he came to see me on the Friday. When he came into my room, I told him he could take a seat in my prayer chair. I don't normally do that, but God wanted to do something at the end of the examination. Again, I asked him if I could pray for him and that's when the Lord started to minister to him. God told me to tell him that he was going to do surgery on him. The Lord said, "You like to heal people's muscles but today I'm going to heal your muscles. I'm going to heal your heart. I'm going to mend your broken heart." The Lord then told me to ask him who the doctor was that was killed that has the same name as he does. Immediately his eyes welled up and he said, "That's my father's twin brother." He told me that his uncle and another doctor were on a decision-making board regarding benefits and salary that were payable to someone who was injured on their job. He said his uncle gave the man a rate that he wasn't pleased with, so he shot him in the head.

The Lord ministered to him and comforted him. I told him it was time to start healing and that his joy would return. Additionally, he would go back to enjoying family time together with his relatives because the surgery was completed. I watched this grown man wept as the lord operated on his heart. I held him in my arms like any mother would and prayed with him through. When he was ready to leave, he gave God thanks, and he thanked me as well.

He testified that he felt a warmth running through his body and that it was a comforting kind of warmth. He then explained, "This is not the norm, I'm the one who normally leaves my patients crying now you the patient, made me cry." Again, I hugged him. I told him no; it was God who made them cry. He visited me another time after that because a storm was coming, and he wanted to make sure I would be safe. To God be the glory!!

We both experienced our miracles, and out of it, came a good friendship. Our God will do exceedingly, abundantly, above, and beyond what we could ask of Him. He is always faithful. And as long as we remain obedient, many will experience the faithfulness of a true and loving God.

Takeaway

Obedience will cause others to experience God's healing power.

Chapter 11
Obeying the God that you know

Yet on another occasion, God again required me to obey a request that started out being emotionally painful for me. A decision of obedience that was very uncomfortable. It started with God showed me a glimpse of a bus leaving my church late one evening with the members of the dance ministry that I was a part of. All I could remember was the brokenness I felt, coupled with the feeling of being unduly punished. That was all I was privy to seeing. Sure enough the occasion presented itself.

The ministry had planned its annual early January retreat. We had an issue with transportation, I spoke with someone I knew about renting us one of his luxury buses for the trip. Being the kindhearted person he was, he let us have the bus free of cost. Everything was in place, I got off work early and the driver hurriedly took me home. As I entered my house, I heard God saying, "Send the driver away, you won't be going with them."

Tears filled my eyes as I turned around to carry out God's instructions. The driver, who was my assistant, and a confidant was very sad too as he was walking me through the arrangement process. I told him God wanted me to go to church. We had a visiting speaker who was doing a week of meeting with us, who coincidentally was used by God to instruct me to enter into a liquid fast for 3 days which would have ended that Friday night. Let me share the humor of this prophecy with you. On the first night of the meeting, the Evangelist told us that God was calling someone into a three-day liquid fast. I immediately responded and told God; "I know for sure You are not speaking to me. You know I would pass out on day one." The young man could not shake the unction of the Word. He kept interjecting it into his message.

The second night he came, and the same thing happened. However, while I was again reassuring God that He was not speaking to me, the Evangelist started to share about drinking lemon grass to sustain oneself through the fast. That caught my attention and then I said to myself "Wow!" He likes the very tea that's my favorite, it was then that I realized that he was speaking to me. I laughed at how I had distanced myself from the wooing of God's spirit. I repented and started my fast the following day which was Wednesday. Little did I know that God was emptying me to fill me with more of Him for a specific assignment. So, here I was on Friday evening closing out my fast with the news that I won't be going on the retreat that I spent the last few weeks anticipating.

As I sadly made my way to the meeting, I saw the bus with the other members of the ministry passing me on another street. I later found out that they were making their way to my house. I hid there for nearly 2 hours hoping they would become frustrated and leave me. Again, I was crying and wondering what I had done wrong. That small glimpse I had seen in reality was now causing me a measure of hurt. When I reached the church, I sat in the corner in the second row. I didn't want anyone to ask me why I was there and not on the trip. I was mad at God, I wouldn't ask Him anything, nor did I position myself to hear from Him. But the Holy Spirit broke forth upon me. So, I had no choice or desire to do anything but to yield to Him. Before long I was interceding for the meeting and the speaker. There was a massive deliverance session that night. I do believe that God was exalted in our midst. Before the service ended a sister came to me and asked how I was going to get to the retreat.

She offered me a ride and said she would pick me up early the next morning. She even gave me a ride home. During the ride home she was sharing how excited she was about going to the retreat. All I wanted to do then was to run to my prayer chair and start a conversation with my Lord. When I finally did that, He told me He had more use for me in intercession at the meeting than at the retreat. He said I should rest because the journey the next morning was a long one. We left very early the next morning and were able to reach our destination during the group's devotion time.

We slipped right in, and before I was fully settled, I was asked to pray. As we prayed, I felt led to walk within the prayer circle we had made. The Holy Spirit then told me to ask a young lady if I could remove the ring from her right thumb. The ring looked like a snake and was coiled around her finger. The minute it was removed there was a demonic manifestation which the Holy Spirit instructed me to cast out.

There were several of those manifestations during the devotion. This was my first time leading in a deliverance session of that magnitude. But in obeying the Lord and going on the liquid fast, I was emptied enough for Him to fill me with more of Him, His love, and His power.

Takeaway

The more we know God, the more we will obey Him. The more we obey Him, we will know His faithfulness.

Chapter 12
Obedience Is as Act of Our Free Will

"If anyone wills to do His will, he shall know concerning the doctrine, whether it is from God or whether I speak on My own authority". John17:7

Many years ago, I heard in my spirit that God would help me to write this book. I always told myself that I would never be able to write an entire book. Yet, the thought that God would help me was being magnified in my thoughts. I also believe that God will honor His word to do that which He says He will do. So, for those of you who might be asking how this walking in Godly obedience works, I am going to try to bring some clarity.

It was only a few minutes ago that a thought entered my mind. "Obedience is an act of our free wills." I pondered on it and realized that it was the heading for this section of the book. I knew that the importance would require some explanation. Hence, I hesitated to start, but I also know the importance of surrendering my will to the prompting of the Holy Spirit. The Bible says our souls have cleaved to the dust. This means we naturally think in ways that suit our desires which might not be in sync with the intent of God. The Apostle Paul, in his letter to the Romans, tells us that surrendering to God in loving obedience is the least we can do as an act of reasonable service to God.

The Contemporary English Version puts this exhortation this way; *"Dear friends, God is good. So, I beg you to offer your bodies to him as a living sacrifice, pure and pleasing. That's the most sensible way to serve God. Don't be like the people of this world, but let God change the way you think. Then you will know how to do everything that is good and pleasing to him.* (Rom 12:1-2 CEV)

While the Message Version for this same scripture gives a very practical explanation of how we can do this, here's what I want you to do with God helping you: *"Take your everyday, ordinary life—your sleeping, eating, going to work, and walking-around life—and place it before God as an offering. Embracing what God does for you is the best thing you can do for him. Don't become so well-adjusted to your culture that you fit into it without even thinking.*

Instead, fix your attention on God. You'll be changed from the inside out. Readily recognize what he wants from you, and quickly respond to it. Unlike the culture around you, always dragging you down to its level of immaturity, God brings the best out of you, develops well-formed maturity in you. (Rom 12:1-2 MSG)

The maturity mentioned here is what will guide us to say a quick and willing obedient "yes" to God. Bearing in mind our delayed obedience is still an act of disobedience. This delay reveals that somewhere in our procrastination was an un-surrendered thought that instructed our will to disobey. It might have been a lack of fully trusting or believing God or His Word. Yet, in His wisdom and Omniscience, God has made room for a repentant will. God fashioned us as tripartite beings having a body, soul, and spirit. This makes us a representation of the unity of the Holy Trinity. The oneness of God manifested in three. All people are identifiable but indivisible. God the Father a reflection of our souls. God the Son a representation of our humanity and God the Holy Spirit represents the part of us that is connected to God. Remember, God blew breath (His Spirit) into man, and man became a living soul. Genesis 2:7 Let's quickly look at how we communicate and respond to God and why Godly obedience is possible. Looking from the outside inward our flesh is world consciousness. It's how we exist and relate to the world around us as we use our five senses and natural faculties. Our spirits make us God-conscious. It is the part of us that is derived from God.

In our spirits, we respond to demons and angels. Our soul is the part of us that houses our will, emotion, and intellect. It makes us relate to the fact that we exist. The soul identifies and acknowledges God through the connection of our spirit with Him. The soul is where choices are made. Our intellect processes what we have heard about God and His Word and leads us to believe unto salvation. When this process is done, our emotions kick in with a response that our will carries out. That's because obedience to God is through faith in Him. *"Faith comes by hearing and hearing by the word of God." (Romans 10:17)* We now realize that when our flesh has dominion over what we think, we will struggle with obeying God. His plan for the salvation of our soul is paramount because our intellect and will can be drawn to the wrong source of knowledge.

The tree of knowledge of good and evil was in the middle of the Garden of Eden, but it was not meant to be the source of man's daily life. Even the simplest act of rejecting God's word is disobedience. Praise be to God, that in His redemption plan, our resurrected body will have a seat of decision that is no longer controlled by our flesh (mind). It is through this spirit and soul existence that we will eternally obey God. Our earthly existence is a rehearsal loaded with choices that will determine our relationship with God. Many Christians tend to see mostly demons with limited angelic encounters.

I personally believe that it's an indication that we are still living below where God wants us to live - I say this because if someone is gifted by God to see in the realm of the spirit- then that person would have the ability to see heavenly angels as well as fallen angels. Seeing only those who exist at the low levels causes me to wonder if we are maximizing our gifts. Remember, as children of God we are seated with Christ in heavenly places. (Ephesians 2:6)

I remember the first angelic encounter that I could recall. I was in the midst of an intercession. I was praying for schools and asking God to send help to the teachers. Immediately, with my eyes still closed, I saw two beings whose hips were above my head. I had to look up. They had on pure white flowing ankle-length gowns with large golden belts. I saw only the sides. I never saw belt buckles, etc. I remember being overshadowed by a great sense of peace, protection, and confident assurance. The funny part about this encounter was that because I had not read anyone's account of seeing angels, I started to shout in my prayers. "The giants are here the giants are here, and they are here to help. " I was so caught up in the moment that it never dawned on me how crazy I must have sounded.

To God be the glory, this experience gave me a more determined resolve to center my emotions down so I can hear the Spirit of God instructing my spirit and soul to do His divine will. In conclusion, we now know there is always a wrestle between our spirit and flesh for our soul. Our will submit to the part of us that is more dominant. Our spirits will lead us to respond to God because God is a Spirit.

Yet, whatever part is ruling will determine how our soul responds. If it's our flesh, our will then causes us to walk in obedience to the dictates of the flesh. We also know that it's our soul that must be saved. It must be brought into submission to God's spirit that lives in us. Once we are living this way, obedience to God will be our more likely response.

Many believers don't realize that most of what we hear starts within our souls without impacting the physical ear. Therefore, we must pay close attention to what enters our souls since our minds cause our emotions to direct our wills. Jesus in His humanity had a will that was in sync with His heavenly father's. *For I have come down from heaven to do the will of God who sent me, **not to do my own will**. And this is the will of God, that I should not lose even one of all those he has given me, but that I should raise them up at the last day. (John 6:38-39 NLT)*

Takeaway

We will obey who or what we submit ourselves to.

Chapter 13
Obeying Instructions That Are Odd

"And this is love: that we walk in obedience to his commands." – (2 John1: 6)

Noted American artist Friedrich Nietzsche said, "There is always madness in love. But there is also always some reason in madness." Most real lovers of God are often viewed by onlookers as (a) freaks, (b) weirdo, (c) strange and (d) sometimes just plain overly. I definitely belong to category e, "All of the above". It just depends on what God asked me to do and who is looking on. You see when we enter a love relationship with our Lord, our obedience will be the outward expression of that love.

Others will see and know for sure that we are driven by a passion that surpasses our own fickle emotions. True love for God will cause us to obey Him when we want to and when we don't want to. When we understand and when we don't understand. When we believe and when we don't believe. One thing I know for sure is that God's ways are past finding out, and He can definitely be trusted to work out something for our good or the good of someone else. Again, God in His benevolence invited me to be an active participant in one of His plans to extend mercy and grace to someone. This happened during the weekend of October 20-21, 2012, when the ferocious storm hurricane Sandy was getting ready to pound New York. We had just arrived home from the church earlier the Sunday evening when I heard God's familiar voice in my spirit, telling me, "Move those flowerpots". Now I must confess, they weren't easy to move but I said to myself, for some reason God wants to move them from where they were. I thought He was preserving the pots as they were sitting at the foot of the steps leading up to our front door. I thought He was just telling me to put them in a safer spot because He knows all things. I was wearing high heels and definitely did not have the best coordinating skills. Anyway, I lifted the first pot and put it where He said right behind a low hedge that was a fencing for the front of the yard. I even had the audacity to kind of give God my nod on the idea. I thought to myself how definitely safe the pot would be there.

The next spot He gave me didn't look so safe, but I said in my mind He knows everything. I obediently placed the second pot on the ground in a small divide that was between our walkway and the driveway that leads to our garage. This driveway has a very steep gradient because our house is at the foot of a hill. By the time I finished doing what I was told by the Holy Spirit, my sisters had already entered the house, so I shared with them what the Lord told me to do. We went about our usual business and before long it was bedtime. Somewhere in the night, the wind started to blow, but not very heavily. It had just started to blow and hadn't yet picked up momentum. I was a-wakened by a heavy threshing sound, like something heavy rolling over a huge pile of dried leaves. I thought that it was the impact of the wind on the trees and even said to myself "My, this wind is blowing heavily." It was only after listening very keenly that I realized somewhere within the threshing sound that there was the sound of an engine being turned over. This made me very curious to know what had been destroyed by the breeze. So, I decided to look out my window, which was right above my bed, to see what was going on. The sound was actually coming from right below my bedroom window. To my surprise, there was a car right across the walkway coming up to the steps. This car somehow managed to tear down the evergreen hedge that was about 3 feet high and was heading straight across the small divide making its way straight for the driveway that led to the garage door. This driveway was almost 5 feet lower than the house's entrance. I could not believe what I was seeing. Had the car not been stopped, the driver would have experienced life-threatening injuries, if not death. The only thing that prevented the car from turning over onto its roof was the large flowerpot that was stuck underneath it. The car could not move. It was stuck- unable to go in any direction. The driver kept trying to put it in reverse. Any wrong move could result in a catastrophe, which I now realize was the enemy's plan. However, it was the other flowerpot that really brought the car to a complete stop. The devil had a plan, but God's plan is greater, and God's plan is a plan of life. A plan of good and not evil.

We called the police and then went downstairs to check on the driver, who was a young man in his early twenties. He was visibly shaken and told us that the car was his aunt's. To God be the glory both he and the car were safe. By now all three of us were weeping and giving God the glory for what He did for this young man. I testified to him about the instructions God had given to me the evening before. We used the opportunity to minister to everyone who was present on the scene. Again, obedience was the key that unlocked God's faithfulness. God's instructions don't always have to sound serious for us to obey. Obeying a simple instruction such as, relocating two flowerpots caused the will of God for this young man's life to be fulfilled.

Takeaway

Loving God and obeying Him are inseparable
"He who has My commandments and keeps them is the one who loves me" John 14:21

Conclusion

*E*very act of Godly obedience gives us the faith to continue walking in more obedience. Each loving response to the will of God, will bring our Heavenly Father pleasure. His gracious response will strengthen us to live beyond our opinions of people's perception of us. Although, Godly obedience won't always lead us to do what is good or right in everyone's eyes, but our call to this walk of loving obedience is anchored in the effectual work of the blood of Jesus Christ His soul cleansing blood will continually cleanse us from the power of sins disobedient hold.

And the work of the Holy Spirit will empower us. Therefore, let us submit in loving obedience to the leading of the Holy Spirit. As The Message Translation says, "*God the Father has his eye on each of you and has determined by the work of the Spirit to keep you obedient through the sacrifice of Jesus. May everything good from God be yours!*" (1 Peter 1:2 MGS)

About the Author

*R*ev. Dr. Lurline Grant is an ordained Elder and Youth Pastor at Her Abiding Presence Evangelistic Ministries Inc. (H.A.P.E.M.) Portchester New York. Elder Lurline is a teacher of God's Word who does so on many different levels whether as a Sunday school teacher to preschoolers or as a Teacher at the International Accelerated Missions (IAM) School in New York. Her love for the Lord and His people is what motivated her to pen this book.

Made in the USA
Middletown, DE
27 October 2023